Active Parenting Today

The Basics

A Guide
For Parents of 2 to 12 Year Olds

By Michael H. Popkin, Ph.D.

To my children, Megan and Ben,
who challenge me to practice what I preach.

Published by Active Parenting Publishers, Inc., Atlanta, Georgia
ISBN 1-880283-06-9

Acknowledgements

Many of the ideas and skills taught in this book come from the work of two great psychologists, Alfred Adler and Rudolf Dreikurs. Other psychologists whose ideas can be learned in Active Parenting are: Carl Rogers, Robert Carkhuff, Thomas Gordon, and Haim Ginott.

I also want to thank three of my own teachers: Professors Ken Matheny, Roy Kern, and Oscar Christensen. They taught me a lot and encouraged me even more.

Thanks also to Lisa Wasshausen, Product Development Manager, and the great Active Parenting staff, Nancy Ballance, Jim Benson, Deb Berg and Jim Polak, for their hard work on this book.

A special thank you to Jennifer Burgin, who encouraged us to write this version of a parent's guide. Jennifer makes things happen.

Finally, Carol Thompson Ruddic did a fine job on the rewrite and revision of this book. She helped me say more with fewer words.

Preface

I started Active Parenting based on two beliefs:

1. Parenting well is important.
2. Parenting well is not easy.

I have worked with many parents over the years. I believe that most love their children. Most want to parent well. The problem is that most parents have never been taught the skills to do this. We act as if parents should just know how to do their job. Yet, with all other jobs, people get training and support.

Now, thanks to people such as your *Active Parenting Today* group leader, this is changing. Parents are coming together to learn better ways to lead their children. You have taken a big step already. You have realized that even if you are already a "good" parent, you can still learn to be a better one.

This book is meant to help you. Use it for the good health of you and your children. And remember, you have an important job. You are a parent!

Michael Popkin
Atlanta, 1993

Table of Contents

Chapter 1
The Active Parent..6

Chapter 2
Courage and Self-Esteem.....................................20

Chapter 3
Understanding Your Child...................................36

Chapter 4
Responsibility..52

Chapter 5
Cooperation...76

Chapter 6
The Active Family..94

Chapter 1

The Active
Parent

In this course, you will learn how to be an "active" parent. Many parents are "reactive." This means they wait until their child does something wrong—then they react. Parents react when they are angry or hurt. This can lead to screaming or hitting.

"Active" parenting also means to **be** active, to get involved with your children. A hug says more than "hello."

We believe the parent should be the leader in the family. In this course we will

■ help you learn what your children need
■ teach you good ways to help your children fill those needs
■ help you enjoy being a parent

What you do and how you do it are important. Your children will be watching you and learning. As you learn, remember, we all make mistakes.

What if you find out you are making mistakes with your children? That's OK. Almost everyone does. You will learn how to change the way you act. Mistakes are for learning. Be gentle with yourself. Do not make yourself feel bad just because you made a mistake.

Children and parents have different jobs. The parent's job is to be a leader in the family. The child's job is to learn. In some ways children and adults are equal. They have an equal right to be treated with respect. They have an equal need to say what they think and feel.

The job of parenting will be easier if you

1. talk with other parents about safe risks children can take in your community

2. join parent groups like church or parent-teacher groups to make a better place for your children to live
3. let your child learn independence gradually, using skills you will learn from this book.

What Kind of Parent Are You?

1. **The Autocratic Parent:** ("The Boss") The Boss is a parent who has all of the control. The Boss is very powerful in the lives of her children. The Boss gives them a reward when they are good. The Boss punishes them when they are bad. Children are told what to do, how to do it, where to do it and when to do it. This worked for our grandparents but does not work well today. The Boss puts limits on children without

giving them freedom. We can show this as a circle. The circle is the limits around the children. This is "limits without freedom."

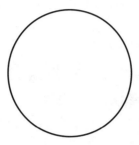

"Limits without freedom."

2. **The Permissive Parent:** ("The Door Mat") The Door Mat parent lets the children do what they want to do. The children do not listen to the parent. The Door Mat parent acts like a rug. He lets the children walk all over him. Children in this family do not feel like they belong. They do not know how to act or work together with others. The Door Mat parent gives freedom to children without setting limits. We can show this as a zig zag. It means there is only freedom. There are no limits to circle the children.

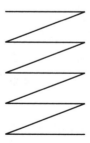

"Freedom without limits."

3. The Democratic/Active Parent: ("The Active") The Active parent is between The Boss and The Door Mat. It is important to give children freedom. It is also necessary to set limits for them. They learn that they have rights and so do other people. The Active (equal) parent "gives freedom to children but sets limits." We can show this as a zig zag in a circle. There is freedom inside the circle of limits.

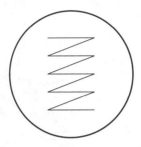

"Freedom within limits."

Reward and Punishment Do Not Always Work

A **reward** is something you give a child for good behavior. Do you pay your children to be good? Do you give them candy, a new sweater, a special treat to try to make them act right? If you do, your child will begin to expect these things all the time.

Punishment is something you do to or take away from a child for bad behavior. How do you treat your children when they are not good? Do you hit them, scream at them, or send them to their room? If you do, your children will become hurt and angry. Your children may start to find ways to get even.

There are many better ways you can work with your children. You will learn more about them later.

What Kind of Child Do You Want?

What is the job of the parent? The parent teaches the child to live in the world. We want kids who will be happy and healthy. What does your child need to know to live in this world?

1. Courage. With courage, kids will be able to handle any of life's problems. They will try, fail and try again until they win. Without courage, children either give up easily or do not try at all.

2. Self-Esteem. This is what we think of ourselves. With self-esteem, your child thinks he can succeed. He does not give up when he fails. He sees himself as a winner. He needs high self-esteem to have courage. This leads to positive behavior in your child.

3. Responsibility. This means your child learns that what he does affects himself and other people. When our children grow up, they will make hundreds of choices. How will their actions affect themselves and others? If they are offered drugs, will they say yes or no? What will they do about sex, crime, drinking and dropping out of school? We must teach them to think before they do anything. What they do will affect their lives and others.

4. Cooperation. Can your child work together with other people? Being part of a team is very important. The child who can work with others has a better chance to be happy and do well in the world. The child who does not learn cooperation may have problems as he grows up. Parents and children should be able to live together peacefully. Parents can not demand respect and love from their children. Parents must earn it.

We Will Help You Teach Your Children To

■ **try even harder when they are afraid (courage)**

■ **think of themselves as winners (self-esteem)**

■ **think before they act (responsibility)**

■ **be able to work together with other people (cooperation)**

Choices

Choice is power. Each of us has the right and the ability to choose. "Freedom within limits" means the child is free to make some choices. This gives each child a sense of power.

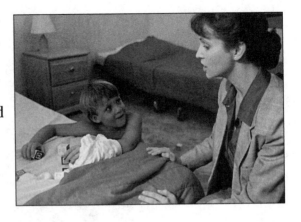

As a parent, you control **what** choices your child can make. This helps guide the child within limits.

Do Not Boss. Give a Choice.

You can give simple choices to young children. In the video, Laura can not convince Zack to wear his shirt. But, when she gives him a choice, the conflict is over.

Laura gave Zack a choice of 2 shirts. Zack picked the shirt he wanted to wear. What if Zack wanted to wear a shirt that was dirty or ragged? Laura could say:

"I am sorry, Zack. That T-shirt is not fit for going out. How about this yellow shirt?"

As children get older, you can give them different choices.

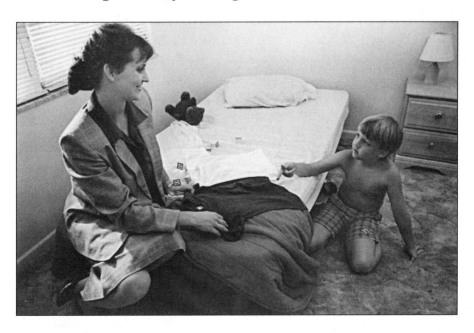

Choices For Children

Child age 2-5:

"Would you like orange juice or apple juice today?"

"Can you put this away yourself or would you like some help?"

"Would you like to take your bath now or after one more song?"

Child age 6-12:

"Do you want to do your homework before or after dinner?"

"Would you like to set the table or help make the salad?"

"Would you like to visit Grandma on Saturday or Sunday?"

Do not make everything a choice. Parents need to guide and direct children. This helps them make good choices.

Home Activity #1 Take Time for Fun

Taking time for fun with your child is very important. It helps build trust. It tells your child that you like him. It also makes discipline easier. You can spend 5 minutes or an hour with him. Here are some things you can do with your child:

1. Read a story

2. Play ball

3. Do a puzzle

4. Sing a song

5. Make popcorn

6. Hug, cuddle, or chase each other

How to have the most fun:

1. Find things you both like to do.

2. Ask your kids what they like to do.

3. Try not to put your children down. Forget your problems. Just have fun together.

Keep a list of the fun things you do each day with your kids. Remember, you can spend 5 minutes, 1 hour, or the whole day with them.

Sharing Fun With Your Kids

Child #1 name_____

What did you do?_____

_____

How did it go?_____

_____

Child #2 name_____

What did you do?_____

_____

How did it go?_____

_____

Child #3 name_____

What did you do?_____

_____

How did it go?_____

_____

Take time for fun. ▶

Choices Activity

Choices I can give my child this week:

Child #1 name_____

Choice _____

_____

What happened? _____

_____

Child #2 name_____

Choice _____

_____

What happened? _____

_____

Child #3 name_____

Choice _____

_____

What happened? _____

_____

Chapter 2

Courage and
Self-Esteem

Courage

We think that courage is one of the most important things you can teach your child. With courage, your child will be able to overcome his fear. Your child will be able to handle life's problems, pain or danger. It is your job to help your child learn courage. One way your child will learn courage is by the way you treat him.

Self-Esteem

Where does courage come from? It comes from a belief in ourselves. We have high "self-esteem" when we believe in ourselves. We like ourselves. We think we can succeed. This gives us the courage to take risks.

When we do not like ourselves, we lose our "self-esteem." We do not think we can succeed. We get discouraged. Our life becomes full of fear.

Your Child Needs Courage and Self-Esteem

The child who "acts bad" does not have courage. He is dis-couraged. Why? Maybe because no one pays attention to him. Maybe no one cares about her. Maybe your child has low self-esteem. Are you telling your kids you do not care? Are you ignoring them? Let's look at how some parents rob their children of courage and self-esteem.

1. **"My kid always gets into trouble."** — If you **expect** that your child will do something wrong, he probably will. If you **expect** your child to fail, she probably will. Children know how you feel by the things you say and do.

 Examples:
"While I am out, you better **not** jump on the bed."

"You will just spill it if you try."

2. **"My kid can not do anything right."** — Why is it hard for your child to do things right? It may be because you do not see the "right" things he does. The only time you notice your child may be when he "acts bad."

Examples:

"See what you have done? I told you, you would spill the milk!"

"When are you going to learn to do things right? You have done this a hundred times. You have not done it right yet."

3. **"Why can't my kid do better?"** — If you expect more from your child than she can give, she will stop trying. She knows she will never please you. The only way for her to make her mark is to do **everything** wrong.

 Examples:

"Look at your brother. He always helps around the house without complaining. Why can't you be more like him?"

"There is no reason you can't make all A's."

4. **"My kids will get hurt if I do not watch over them."** — Do you help them out every time they make a mistake? Then they will always come to you when things go wrong. They will never learn to stand on their own two feet. They will be afraid of life.

Examples:

"Let me do that for you—it will be faster."

"You should not do that. Wait until you get bigger."

When children hear negative things about themselves, they believe them. They learn to have negative feelings. This leads to low self-esteem and lack of courage.

Give Your Child Courage and Self-Esteem

Here are ways you can encourage your children:

Expect The Best
Do not look for the mistakes. Expect the best of your child. Help your child find out what she can do. Help her see the best in herself.

1. Give your child something to do and expect she will do it right.

 Examples:

"You can have a dog if you agree to feed, walk, and care for him."

"You have been doing such a good job of helping me make your bed. Tomorrow morning, I am going to let you make it all by yourself."

25

2. Ask your kids what they think. Do they know how to do something really well? Do they know a lot about cars or music? Ask them what they think about different things. It helps them feel good about themselves.

 Examples:

"I like that new game you got for your birthday. Will you teach me to play?"

"How can we keep these toys from getting broken?"

3. Try not to do too much for your child. Remember, he will find some things hard to do. You may be able to do it faster or you may feel sorry for him. But doing it for him will not help him.

 Example:

Johnny is 3 years old and Mother still feeds him. He makes such a mess with his food. It is faster and easier for Mother to feed him. Maybe, someday, he will learn to eat properly.

When you give too much help, he thinks he can not do it by himself. What happens? The next time he tries to do something hard, he will give up. He will let Mother do it for him.

What you can say to help your child:

"Keep trying. I know you can do it. Just a little more and you will have it."

Find What Is Right About Your Child

Talk about all the things your children do right. They will do them more often. Here are some ways to do this:

1. Catch them doing something good. It can be a small, simple thing. Praise them. Thank them for their help. Every time you **notice** them, it is important.

Examples:
"We really had a good time at dinner tonight. Your manners were great. We will go out to eat again soon."

"I like the way you shared your orange with Jack."

"Thank you for helping with the dishes."

2. Watch for them to do better. Do not expect them to be perfect. Remember, a baby must crawl before it can walk. Your child will learn in small steps, too. Praise each step he learns. Each step is hard for your child. When you praise him, it is easier to learn the next step. Do not give up on him, even if he fails.

 Examples:
"You are getting better in your reading. I can hear the difference."

"You really tried hard."

3. Look at what your child is already doing well. Then build on that. Add a new step. Work on it until your child has learned it. Then add another step. With your praise, your child will want to learn more.

 Examples:
"You did a good job of putting on your shirt. Now let's start to learn to button it."

"Great job! This room is really starting to look good."

Love Your Child - The Good and The Bad

Children need to feel they are important. They must also grow up **liking** themselves. You must show them love, no matter what they do or say. Even when they do all the wrong things, they are still good kids. Here are some ways you can tell them how you feel.

1. Your child gets an "A" or wins an award. Is that the only time you show you love her? Winning prizes has nothing to do with your love for her. It is better to be proud of her for trying.

 Examples:

"It is more important to play your best than to win."

"I am glad you enjoy learning."

2. There are no bad children. Sometimes they just "act bad." When you talk to your child, talk about how he acted. You still love your child, even when he makes mistakes. But your child may not know this. He may think he is bad because he "acted bad." You must show him the right way to think.

Examples:

"When I get angry at you, it does not mean I do not love you. It means you did something I did not like."

"I see you made a mistake. Well, let's see what you can learn from it."

3. Each child is special. How can you show her she is special? Be interested in what she does. Show her how you feel by the things you say and do. Love her for who she is.

Examples:

"You are a neat kid, you know it?"

"I like you."

Learning To Be Independent

Children must learn to do things themselves. They can not expect other people's help all the time.   They need to

- learn to do the things they can do
- learn to ask for help when they need it
- learn to give help when someone asks

1. Let kids do things for themselves. Step by step, children learn to control their lives. They learn to feel good about themselves. Let them learn at their own pace. Do not push. Tell them you will help, if they need it. Your kids learn to be independent when you give them choices.

 Examples:

"Would you like cereal or toast for breakfast?"

"Do you want to dress yourself, or do you want me to help?"

2. Children must learn they are part of a family. As they grow, they also learn they are part of the world. It can be fun to be part of a group with everyone working together.

 Examples:

"Would you like to make cookies with us?"

"We are all going out to dinner and you are coming, too."

Home Activity #2 A "Good Job" Letter

Saying good things to your child is very important. But you can also write it on paper. Then your kids can keep your words with them.

This week, write a letter to one or all of your children.

Tips:

- Write about how much better they are doing.
- Be honest—do not say your kids are doing better if they are not.
- Write what they have done right.
- Tell them how they have helped you and others.

 Example:

Dear Johnny:

We were walking by your bedroom this morning. We saw that you had made your bed without being told. We are so happy that you are keeping your bed neat. We all want our house to be a special place to live. We are so glad you are helping out.

Thanks,
Mom & Dad

Practice saying something nice to your kids this week. Make a mark each time you say something positive to your children. When you encourage them, they gain courage. Then they act better.

Child's name	Day	Make a ✓ for each good thing you say								

VIDEO PRACTICE 1

Let's look at the 4 scenes in the video. Pretend you are the child. What would you think, feel, do?

Scene #1: Ben and the cereal

What would you **think** if you were that child? _____

_____

_____

_____

How would you **feel** if you were that child? _____

_____

_____

_____

What would you **do** if you were that child? _____

_____

_____

_____

Scene #2: Ben and the cereal

What would you **think** if you were that child? _____

_____

_____

_____

How would you **feel** if you were that child? _____

_____

_____

_____

What would you **do** if you were that child? _____

_____

_____

_____

Scene #3: Janelle and her homework

What would you **think** if you were that child? _____

_____

_____

_____

How would you **feel** if you were that child? _____

_____

_____

_____

What would you **do** if you were that child? _____

_____

_____

_____

Scene #4: Janelle and her homework

What would you **think** if you were that child? _____

_____

_____

_____

How would you **feel** if you were that child? _____

_____

_____

_____

What would you **do** if you were that child? _____

_____

_____

_____

Value the child as he or she is.   ▶

Chapter 3

Understanding
Your Child

Sometimes it is hard to understand your children. Did your parents ever say to you:

- "I just do not understand you!"
- "Why do you do things like that?"
- "Where have I failed?"

They were saying they could not understand the way you acted. Let's see how and why your children act the way they do.

What Do Children Need?

Here are four things your children need every day. These are called the goals of their behavior.

Contact
(the **goal** to belong)

Power
(the **goal** to control their lives)

Protection
(the **goal** to feel safe)

Withdrawal
(the **goal** to rest and be calm)

1. Contact. We all have a need to touch, talk, and belong with other human beings. It starts when we are babies. As we grow, the **need** (goal) is still there. Even as adults, we touch, talk, and get attention. That is why we join clubs, go to parties, get married and have friends. A child has this need. Parents must be sure kids get enough contact so they do not feel alone.

2. Power. We all want things to go our way. We want the power to make things **happen**. The best way for us to get power is through learning. The more we know, the more power we have. We want our children to become strong so they can control their lives. They become strong by learning about the world.

3. Protection. We all want to feel safe, both in our families and in the world. Our children should not be afraid of anyone in the family. They should not feel afraid of neighbors and friends.

4. Withdrawal. We need to take time out each day to rest and be calm. Children have a lot of energy. This energy keeps them going all day. They need to take time each day to be calm. This will let them understand themselves better.

Acting "Good" - Acting "Bad"

We believe there are no good or bad children. There are children who feel good about themselves. There are children who do not feel good about themselves. How a child feels affects the way the child acts.

What To Do When a Child "Acts Bad"

Your child does something you do not like. Ask yourself, "Why is he doing this?" "What does she want?" Now look at how you feel. Do you feel annoyed, angry, hurt or helpless? Here are some things you can do when your child "acts bad":

Child's goal of contact: Children want to belong. If they are ignored, they feel alone and afraid. Sometimes, your child tries to get attention from you at the wrong time or by doing something "bad." The child is being a pest. **You feel annoyed.** Maybe you scold or punish. This gives the child what she wants: contact. She may stop for a moment. But soon she tries again.

What you can do: Give the child a lot of attention some other time. Act more. Talk less.

Example: Johnny's mother was busy in the kitchen. Suddenly, she heard a loud crash. Johnny had broken a potted plant in the living room. Johnny was trying to get his mother's attention. He knew she would come running when she heard the noise. Mother had Johnny clean up the mess. Later that evening, she spent an hour with Johnny. She talked to him, played with him and gave him hugs.

B **Child's goal of power:** If children are always told what to do, they feel helpless. That means they do not feel they can make things happen. They do not feel they belong. So when the parent tells the child to do one thing, the child does something different. **The parent gets angry.** The child gets worse. Parent and child are in a "power struggle."

What you can do: You should walk away. Both you and the child need time to calm down. Do not fight and do not give in. Wait until you are both calm before you talk to your child.

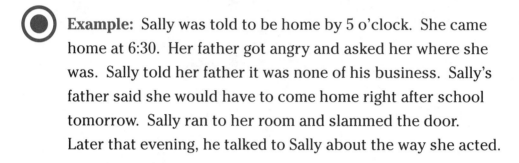

Example: Sally was told to be home by 5 o'clock. She came home at 6:30. Her father got angry and asked her where she was. Sally told her father it was none of his business. Sally's father said she would have to come home right after school tomorrow. Sally ran to her room and slammed the door. Later that evening, he talked to Sally about the way she acted.

Child's goal of protection: Your child may be feeling hurt or afraid. She wants you to know that you hurt her. She wants you to know she does not feel safe. One way she can show you is by hurting you. **Then you feel hurt, too.** The child sees this and keeps on trying to hurt you.

What you can do: Do not show your hurt or anger. Show love. Do not try to hurt her because she hurt you.

Example: Mary and her mother had a fight last night. In the morning she said to her mother, "I hate you. I only love Daddy. I do not love you." Mary's mother almost started to cry. She almost said something hurtful to her child. Instead, she told Mary how much she loved her. Later that day, she talked to Mary about what happened.

Child's goal of withdrawal: Is your child spending a lot of time alone in his room? Does he spend any time with other family members? Does he always say, "Just leave me alone"? Is he afraid to try new things? Your child is not feeling "good enough." He is feeling like he can not do anything right. **You feel**

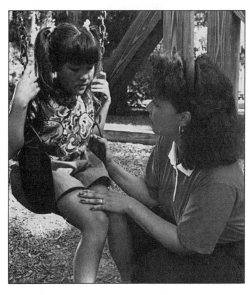

helpless. You do not know what to do. You try to talk to your child. He does not want to talk. He does not want to do anything. He wants to be left alone.

What you can do: Be patient. Keep trying to talk to your child. Be loving. Find out what your child likes the best. Then build on that interest. Help him find things he can do well. Then build on those strengths.

Example: Every day, Mark comes home from school and goes straight to his room. The only time he comes out is for dinner and to watch TV. When Mark's father asks him how school was, Mark says, "Fine." Mark's father asks if he wants to play basketball in the backyard. Mark says no. Then he asks Mark if he wants to go to a movie. Mark says, "Leave me alone."

43

Mark goes into his room and slams the door. His father does not give up. He knows that Mark loves old cars. Mark has pictures of old cars all over his room. Mark's father asks Mark if he wants to go to an auto show.

Parents and Anger

Some people say anger is natural. But anger can also be harmful. It can lead us to say and do things that are hurtful.

How can we use our anger the right way?

Sometimes we really want something. But we can not get it. We get angry. Our anger says to us:

"Act! Don't just sit there. Get up and do something." If we act right away, before we blow up, we can solve the problem. This keeps the problem from getting worse.

How can we act on anger?

We can do it in three ways:

1. Try to change what is happening.

Example: You have told your child to call if he is going to be late. When he does not call and shows up an hour late, you are very angry. Tell him how you feel about the way he acted. Tell him what you would like him to do about it.

"When you do not call, I feel worried and angry. We agreed you would call when you are going to be late. Please keep your promises." Getting angry and yelling does not change how your child acts. Talking to him quietly and firmly will help.

2. What made you angry? Make it less important.

Example: Your child refuses to take a bath. Maybe taking a bath every day is less important. You and your child feeling good about each other may be more important.

3. Change what you want.

Example: Talk to your child. Tell her what you want. Find out what your child wants. Then decide on something you both can live with.

Helping Children Use Their Anger

Children often show their anger by shouting, crying, and hitting. How can you help them use their anger better?

1. You can show them how to do it. You are angry. Do you

- shout?
- say hurtful things?
- hit someone?
- get grumpy or silent?

If you do, your child may do the same thing. You can show him a better way by how you act. You can also talk to him about it.

 Examples: "You have the right to feel angry. But in our family, we do not scream and blame other people. We try to find a way to make things better."

"I can see you are angry. Can you tell me with words instead of hitting?"

2. Do not try to show them your power. Walk away from them. When you are not there, they have no one to fight with. But do not give in to them. They will soon find another and better way to get what they want. They will learn that getting angry does not get them what they want.

Example: Your child demands a cookie before dinner. You've explained that he'll have to wait till after dinner for the cookies. He starts crying and falls on the floor yelling. You leave the room until he calms down.

3. Give your child a choice.

 Example: After 5 minutes your child is still screaming for a cookie. What do you do? Give your child a choice: He can stop screaming and have the cookie after dinner or he can keep screaming and not get the cookie at all.

4. Give your kids the chance to say what they want. Ask them for ideas before you make a decision. They will feel more in control and powerful.

 Example: Does your child give you a hard time when you go to the store? Tell him he can pick out the cereal and the fruit. Listen to his ideas. Ask him why he picked that kind of cereal or fruit. Let him know his decisions are important to you.

Home Activity #3 Teaching Your Child

One of the most important things kids learn is how to take care of themselves. Here are some steps you can follow to help them learn:

1. Help your child want to learn. Tell her how important her help is to the family.

Example: "The family needs your help in folding clothes."

2. Pick a time when you are not in a hurry. Your child will be slow at first and make mistakes. Go slow and be patient.

3. Show your child how to do it right. Talk slowly. Explain what you are doing while you are doing it.

 Example: "You hold the toothbrush in your hand like this."

4. Let your child try. Do not expect your child to do things perfectly the first time. Be gentle about mistakes. Praise him for the parts he does right. Your child is learning each time he does it.

5. Work together. You can work along with her for a short time after she has learned the skill. This is a wonderful time to spend together.

6. Praise your child. Tell him he is doing a good job.

● Example: "You worked really hard setting the table. Thanks."

7. Give your child choices.

● Example: "Would you like to set the table or clear the table after dinner?"

8. Make it fun. Turn on the radio, sing a song, or make a game of it.

On the following page are some skills you can teach your child this week.

Teaching New Skills

- **Putting toys away**
- **Dressing himself**
- **Riding a bike**
- **Folding clothes**
- **Setting the table**
- **Playing basketball**

New Skills

Child #1 name _____

What skill did you teach? _____

_____

What happened?_____

_____

_____

Child #2 name _____

What skill did you teach? _____

_____

What happened?_____

_____

_____

Child #3 name _____

What skill did you teach? _____

_____

What happened?_____

_____

_____

VIDEO PRACTICE 1

Video #2: Janelle

How is the parent feeling? _____

What is the child's goal? _____

What is Dad's parenting style? _____

_____

Video #4: Zack

How is the parent feeling? _____

What is the child's goal? _____

What is Mom's parenting style? _____

_____

Video #6: Jade

How is the parent feeling? _____

What is the child's goal? _____

What is Mom's parenting style? _____

_____

Video #8: Ramon

How is the parent feeling? _____

What is the child's goal? _____

What is Dad's parenting style? _____

_____

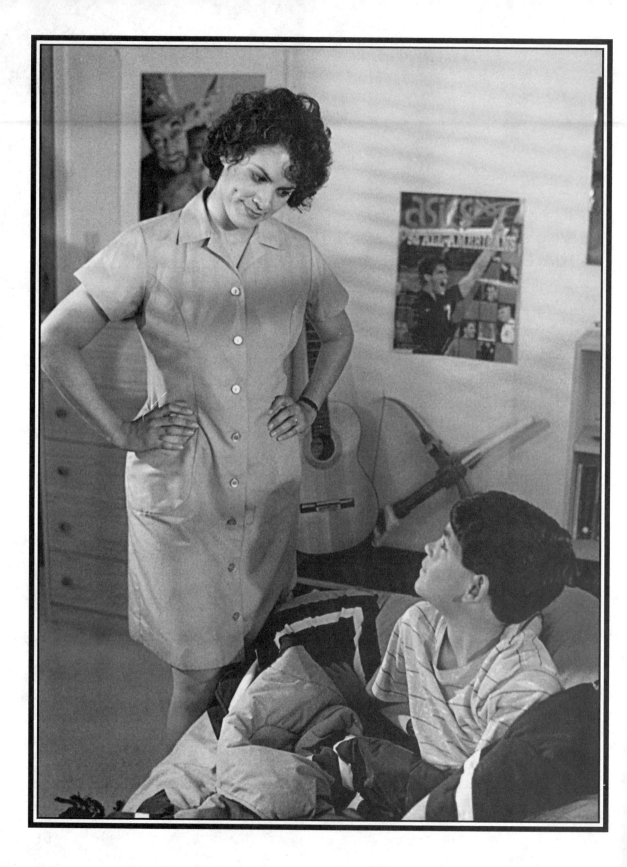

Chapter 4

Responsibility

What Is Responsibility?

Alan was 27 years old. He had never had a job in his life.
His parents took care of him. They gave him money and a
place to live. One day his parents told him to find a job or
move out of the house. After 10 weeks, Alan still did not have
a job. When his parents started to pack his suitcase, Alan got
scared. He had never learned to do things for himself. How
could he possibly find a job? As usual, his father helped him.
He called a friend who got Alan a job driving a dump truck.
The hours and the pay were good.

One day Alan wrecked the truck. He backed it down a hill
where it turned over. When his boss asked him why he did it,
Alan said, "Nobody told me not to."

Responsibility means: When we make choices, we must be
prepared to live with whatever happens.
Some choices we make every day are:

- Do we wash our clothes or wear them dirty?
- Do we keep our teeth clean or let them stay dirty?
- Do we eat fruits and vegetables or junk food?

Each time we choose, something happens. The things that
happen are called **consequences**.

 Examples:
If you wear clean clothes, the **consequences** are

- you look good
- more people like to be with you
- people tell you how nice you look

If you wear dirty clothes, the **consequences** are

- you do not look as good
- some people do not like to be with you
- some people may even make fun of the way you look

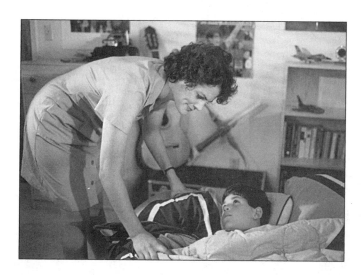

If you clean your teeth each day, the **consequences** are

- your breath smells nice
- your teeth are bright and clean
- your teeth stay healthy
- you do not have to go to the dentist as often

If you do not clean your teeth each day, the **consequences** are

- your breath smells bad
- your teeth look yellow and rotten
- your teeth will start to fall out

So, each time you choose, something happens. It does no good to blame others for what happens to you. You made it happen by what you did. You can not blame the dentist if your teeth fall out. You made a choice not to brush your teeth.

But we must remember that we all make mistakes. What if we make the wrong choice? That is OK, if we admit we made the mistake. We can learn from our mistakes. We can learn to do things differently the next time.

When Kids Make Mistakes

Our kids will make mistakes as they grow up. We have to be careful not to blame them or punish them. What we can do is

- have the child understand he made a mistake
- explain that what happened (**consequences**) was because of what the child did
- explain that when the **consequences** are good, the child has learned to make good things happen
- show that when the **consequences** are unpleasant, the child must learn to make a different choice the next time

Let your child make choices—but within limits.

 Examples:

Child age 2-5:

"Would you like to hear a story or listen to a song?"

"Can you make your bed by yourself or would you like some help?"

"Would you like peanut butter or chicken for your sandwich?"

Child age 6-12:

"Would you like to help me do the grocery shopping?"

"Do you want to have a picnic this Saturday or see a movie?"

"You are able to get up by yourself each morning. We think you will be able to decide when you should go to bed."

But—do not make **everything** a choice. Children need firm but calm decisions from parents.

How To Handle Problems

Who does the problem belong to?
If there is a problem, who does the problem belong to? Not all problems are "owned" by the parent. When your child owns the problem, let him decide how he wants to handle it. Here is how to tell who owns a problem:

- ■ Who talked about the problem first?
- ■ Who was upset by the problem first?
- ■ Who has the consequences from the problem?

Example:
Children are very noisy at a restaurant. This is the **parent's problem**. Why? Because the parent is eating in a public place. The children are disturbing the parent and the other people in the restaurant.

What Does The Parent Do Next?

Ask Politely

Parents do not need to be "tough" all of the time. Children can change their behavior if they are asked gently. Try to be polite the next time you ask your child to do something. Listen to your tone of voice and what you say.

Example:

"Honey, please do me a favor. Bring your dishes to the sink when you are finished eating."

If your child does what you ask, thank him for his help. What happens if your child forgets the next time? Remind him in a friendly way.

Example:

"Honey, I see you forgot to put your dishes in the sink. Please come get them."

What happens if your child does not listen to these gentle requests? You will need to use a stronger message.

"I" Message

The parent uses an "I" message. Here is how it works:
"When you are noisy at the restaurant, I feel annoyed because
I spend most of my time calming you down. I would like you
to talk quietly." Here is how to make an
"I" message:

When you _____

I feel _____

because _____ .

I would like you to _____ .

Consequences

There are some
consequences that happen
whether the parent wants
them to or not. These are
called **natural
consequences**. Some
natural consequences can
be good teachers.

 Examples:
When a child leaves his bike
out in the rain, the chain
rusts.

When a child forgets to wear a jacket outside, she gets cold.

When letting natural consequences teach, do not get in the way. Do not say, "I told you so."

Some natural consequences hurt too much to use
for teaching.

Examples:

When a child touches a hot iron, he will get burned.

When a child plays in a busy street, she may run in front of a car and get hurt.

Sometimes parents can use **logical consequences** to teach. These are consequences that happen because the parents make them happen.

Examples:

What happens when Danny comes home late for supper? He eats cold food alone. He must clean up his own dishes.

What happens when Susan does not pick up her toys? She is not allowed to play with her special game. Or she is not allowed to watch TV.

Parents should be firm and friendly when using consequences.

How To Use Logical Consequences To Teach

1. Give kids a choice about what will happen.

 Examples:

"You may sit at the table and eat quietly or you may leave and go to your room."

"When you have finished your homework, then you may watch TV."

"When you finish your supper, then you may have dessert."

"Tom, when you have cut the grass, then you may go swimming."

Bad ways to give choices:

"Kathy, stop that noise or else you will go to your room."

"Tom, you can not go swimming until you cut the grass."

"You are not going to watch TV until you do your homework."

2. Ask the child to help set consequences. Make children a part of the process. You have a better chance of getting their cooperation. If the child has no suggestions, you should have one. It is important to ask her.

 Example:

"Kathy, I still have a problem with your toys all over the living room floor. What can we do about this problem?"

3. All consequences should be logical. The consequences should make sense to the child. They should be connected to the way the child acted. If they make sense to the child, she learns how to change her behavior. If they do not make sense, she sees it as punishment.

Examples:

Not logical:
"Come in to dinner now or you can not watch TV tonight."
Logical:
"Come in to dinner now or you will miss it."

Not logical:
"Play quietly while I work or I am not taking you to the movie."
Logical:
"Play quietly so I can finish my work.   If I finish my work, I will be able to take you to the movie."

Not logical:
"Stop fighting or you will both get a spanking."
Logical:
"Stop fighting or you will have to play in separate rooms."

4. Only give choices you can live with. What works for one family may not work for another. You, as the parent, decide which choices to give.

 Example:
Your child forgets to wash the dishes. You might say:
"If the dishes are not washed, I will leave them in the sink."

What happens when you have no clean dishes left? Try serving the next meal on the table with no forks or spoons. If this is too messy for you, use other choices.

5. Use a firm and calm voice. Do not get angry. Do not sound unsure of yourself. Be firm and calm. The **tone** of your voice should say: "You had a choice. You made your choice. Now, this is what is going to happen. You may not like the consequence. But, it was your choice. I still love you. I am here to help you grow."

6. Give the choice once. Then act! Your child must see that once he makes a choice, he owns the consequence. The consequence can be good or not so good. It depends on what choice he makes. Your child will learn only if you do what you say you will do.

Example:
Mom says, "Kathy, you can either play quietly here in the living room or go to your room to play alone." Kathy keeps talking and laughing loudly. Mom says, "I see you have decided to play in your room. Bye. See you later."

Kathy does not leave. Mom holds her hand firmly but kindly and takes her into her room. Kathy's crying or shouting should not change what Mom does. Kathy now understands what will happen if she is given the same choices again.

7. Children will test you. You give your child choices, but she still misbehaves. Why? She is testing you. Are you **really** going to leave the dirty dishes in the sink? When she finds out you will **do** what you **say**, she will stop testing.

8. Give the child a chance to try again later. You want the child to learn what will happen from the consequences.

Example:
Kathy was taken to her room to play. After 10 minutes, Mom asks her if she wants to come back to the living room. Kathy says yes. Mom says, "You must have decided to play quietly."

Kathy does not play quietly when she comes back to the living room. Then Mom must be prepared to give her the same consequences. She holds Kathy's hand firmly but kindly and takes her back to her room. She says to Kathy, "I see you have decided to play in your room instead of the living room."

Let the child experience the consequences a little longer. Let her stay in her room for 15 minutes instead of 10. If she comes back into the living room again but does not play quietly, the same thing happens. She is taken back to her room. This time she stays a little longer. Eventually, Kathy will learn from the consequences and make a different choice.

Remember

1. Give kids a choice.
2. Ask the child to help set consequences.
3. All consequences should be logical.
4. Only give choices you can live with.
5. Use a firm and calm voice.
6. Give the choice once. Then act!
7. Children will test you.
8. Give the child a chance to try again.

Mutual Respect

Sometimes parents get angry and use consequences to punish the child. If you do this, the child will not learn the lessons he needs to learn.

■ Do not use an angry voice or look angry.

■ If possible, talk to the child about the problem. Ask her what she thinks the consequences should be.

■ Be sure the consequences make sense. Johnny did not brush his teeth. Dad said he could not play with his friends for a week. Does the consequence make sense?

We want our children to respect us. Parents must earn respect. The best way to earn respect is to show respect. How do you do that? Listen to how you talk to your children. What tone of voice are you using? What words are you saying? How are your children reacting to what you are saying? Do they look like they respect you? Or do they look hurt, angry, or afraid?

Treat your children the same way you want them to treat you. Talk to your children the same way you want them to talk to you. Do you want them to say those things to you? Do you want them to shout at you?

Treating your child with respect shows you care about him as a person. ▶

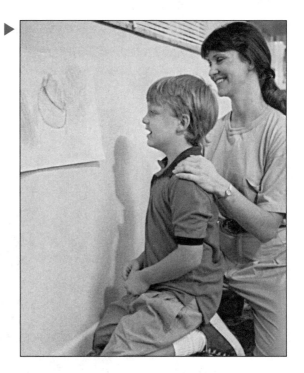

Home Activity #4 Positive "I" Messages

"I" messages are easy for children to hear. They are clear, firm and calm ways to talk to your children. Use "I" messages to correct behavior or to encourage good behavior.

In the video, Laura tries to teach her son, Zack, not to draw on the wall. She uses a logical consequence. Then she uses a positive "I" message. Here is how to put together a positive "I" message.

1. Say what you **like**: "I really like the way you picked up your clothes."

2. Say how you **feel**: "I feel good that you heard what I said about keeping your room clean."

3. Tell them **why**: "Putting your clothes in the laundry means you have more room to play."

4. Offer **to do** something **for them**: "Now that your room is clean, we can play a game."

You do not need to use every step of the "I" message. Telling your child what you like (Step 1) is a good way to encourage her. Use your own words so your message sounds natural.

A Problem From Your Family

I like_____

I feel_____

_____

Why_____

_____

We can _____

What happened?_____

_____

What did you like about it? _____

_____

Will it be different next time? How?_____

_____

VIDEO PRACTICE 1

Whose problem is it? Or who "owns" the problem?

Scene #1: Laura and Zack - phone

Whose problem is it? _____

_____

Why? _____

_____

_____

Scene #2: Laura and Zack - shoes

Whose problem is it? _____

_____

Why? _____

_____

_____

Scene #3: Kathi and Jade - swing

Whose problem is it? _____

_____

Why? _____

_____

_____

Scene #4: Jose, Ramon and Sara - kicking

Whose problem is it? _____

_____

Why? _____

_____

_____

Scene #5: Think of a problem from your own family

Whose problem is it? _____

_____

Why? _____

_____

_____

What happened? _____

_____

_____

"I" Messages

Example:

You have a 10 year old son. He has been making a lot of noise while playing.
You are getting a terrible headache. You have told him twice to play quietly.
He has gotten louder.

Write an "I" message for your son.

I have a problem with _____

I feel _____

because _____

Will you please _____

     or

I would like _____

Now, think of a problem from your family. This should be a problem you "own." Write an "I" message you can use at home. Try this "I" message this week to solve the problem.

When _____

I feel _____

because _____

Will you please _____

    or

I would like _____

What happened?

What happened when you gave your child your "I" message? _____

_____

How do you feel about your "I" message?_____

_____

Would you do it a different way next time? _____

_____

VIDEO PRACTICE 2

We will look at 5 scenes. Can you find anything wrong with the logical consequence used? Can you think of a **better** logical consequence to use?

Scene #1: Ramon oversleeping

What was wrong with the logical consequence? _____

_____

What would be a better logical consequence? _____

_____

Scene #2: Ramon oversleeping

What was wrong with the logical consequence? _____

_____

What would be a better logical consequence? _____

_____

Scene #3: Janelle skating in street

What was wrong with the logical consequence? _____

_____

What would be a better logical consequence? _____

_____

Scene #4: Ben not eating his peas

What was wrong with the logical consequence? _____

_____

What would be a better logical consequence? _____

_____

Scene #5: Jade not returning art supplies

What was wrong with the logical consequence? _____

_____

What would be a better logical consequence? _____

_____

A Problem From Your Family

Now think of a problem that is yours. You "own" this problem. Write the problem here: _____

_____

What kind of logical consequence would be good for this problem? Write down what you would say to your child. _____

_____

_____

What choices would you give your child? _____

_____

_____

What consequences? _____

_____

_____

Chapter 5

Cooperation

What is cooperation? It is working together with other people. It is helping out in the family. It is wanting to help each other. The first step in teaching your kids cooperation is talking to each other.

Example:

Let us say your child has a problem. He may try to work it out on his own. He may succeed or he may fail. But he should not feel he is alone with his problem. How do you help your child? Get him to talk to you. Find out about the

problem. Then help him find ways to handle the problem successfully. Do not do it for him. Give him ideas of what he can do. Show him that 2 people can work together to find an answer.

When you talk to your child, try to make your words match your feelings. If they do not, your child will get a **mixed message**.

Example:

Your words say "I am not angry."
Your voice and face say "I will be angry if you do not do what I say."

Then your child will not know what you mean or what he should do.

How Do We Talk to Our Children?

The best and easiest way is to **listen** first.

Example:
Matt is very angry. He is shouting and crying. Some of the things he is saying are ugly and cruel. Matt's Dad is calm and listens to **what** he is saying. He listens to **how** Matt is talking. Dad does not say, "Don't talk back to me" or "Stop complaining." But he does say, "I can see you are very angry. After you calm down, we will talk about it."

Parents and children must talk together about the problem. Decide who "owns" the problem. Ask yourself, "Whose problem is it?" Then help your child work it out.

Example:
Your child complains that another child does not like her. Whose problem is it? Yours or your child's? The problem belongs to the child. **Why?** Kids have relationships with other children. They need to learn how to relate to them on their own.

When it is the child's problem, she must handle her own problem. Not alone, but with the help of her parents. They do this together by talking. This is called communication.

How Can Parents Help?

Here are 5 ways:

1. Listen with your eyes as well as your ears. Does your child look angry, sad or hurt? Listen with your heart. Can you hear sadness or hurt in his voice? Try not to talk too much. This says to your child, "It is OK to talk about your feelings. I will listen to what you have to say."

Can you listen while you watch TV? Can you listen while you are cooking? Not very well. You need to sit down with your child and really listen. This makes your child feel important. Your child feels that you care. Your child knows you want to help.

You do not have to listen in total silence. You can say simple things like "I see" or "Yes, I understand." But if you do not understand, say, "Are you saying that Billy took the toy and the teacher blamed you?" You are saying back to her what she told you.

2. Listen to what your child is feeling. Does he sound angry? Hurt? Sad? Ashamed? It is important for children to express their feelings. There are no wrong feelings. Some are unpleasant and do not make us feel good. But feelings are not wrong or right.

Many children are afraid of their feelings. Help them know that it is OK to feel things. But they can not always act them out.

Example:

A child feels angry and punches another child. This is acting out his feelings. We teach children to talk it out:

"I do not like it when you take my toy away from me. I'm mad."

3. Help your child understand his feelings. Tell him what you think he is feeling.

Examples:

Child: "I hate Billy. He took my toy."
Parent: "I can see you are angry at Billy because he took your toy."

Child: "Jane is moving away and I'll never see her again."
Parent: "You are sad because your best friend is moving away."

Child: "I'm not going to school. Those kids are so big."

Parent: "It sounds like you are afraid of the bigger kids in your class."

There are many words that you can use to describe feelings. Sometimes we find it hard to think of them. Listed here are some words you may find helpful.

Words for pleasant feelings:

proud	cheerful	understanding	glad
calm	excited	loving	surprised
brave	happy	joyful	pleased

 Examples:

"It sounds like you are very **excited**."

"You were **brave** when we were at the doctor's office."

Words for unpleasant feelings:

afraid	shy	hateful	angry
tired	ashamed	hurt	unhappy
jealous	worried	lonely	disappointed

 Examples:
"I know you are **disappointed** that you did not win."

"You sound **angry**."

4. Help your child decide what to do. Kids need to learn how to solve their problems. What can they

do? What will happen when they do those things? What will be the consequences? You can say, "All right, Susan, what can you do about that? What else can you try?" It is better if the child tries to think of her own actions. If she can not think of an action, you can offer a suggestion: "Maybe you could talk to John the next time that happens."

Sometimes it helps when you share an experience you had as a child: "I remember when I was 10. I had a friend named Bobby. He did the same thing John did to you. I felt angry, too."

After you and your child decide on what she can do, ask, "What do you think will happen if you do that?"

But let your child decide what she will do. Try not to tell her what you think is best. She must learn to take responsibility.

5. What happens when you finish talking? Ask your child what he has decided to do. Ask when he is going to do it. Do not push. Be gentle. After he has acted, you can ask, "How did it go? What happened?"

By doing this, you build a strong bond between you and your children. They learn that you care. They begin to trust you. They will learn to come to you to work out problems. They learn to think first, then act.

Remember:

If there is a problem, find out who owns the problem.

1. If the problem belongs to the parent
    - first ask politely
    - if necessary send an "I" message
    - if that doesn't work, use consequences

2. If the problem belongs to the child
    - let the child handle it
    - help the child by talking with him

3. If the problem can not be handled by child or parent
    - deal with the problem in the family meeting

Making Bedtime Special

Young children need to know that certain things happen at certain times. When they have some structure in their lives, they feel safe and secure. But too much structure can be as bad as not enough structure.

Bedtime seems to be a problem for many parents. The best way to make this better is to start a bedtime routine. Do the same things each night—step by step. Bedtime should be a fun time for your child. Include him in the things you do. Here is a suggestion for a bedtime routine:

1. **Start with a bath.** Try to make it fun and playful. Listen to music or put toys in the bathtub. You can even play make-believe games with soap suds.

2. **Brushing teeth.** Do this after the bath. If this is not fun for your child, try saying things like: "You are doing such a good job. I like the way you open your mouth wide. Can you open as wide as a lion?"

3. Bedtime story. This is usually the favorite part of bedtime. You can read a story or tell a story. This is also a quiet time to share. Talk about what happened that day. Talk about what is going to happen tomorrow. Other special routines may be:

- prayer
- back rub
- a special song you sing each night
- hugs and kisses before your child closes his eyes
- saying "I love you" just before turning out the light

Showing Love

All children want love. Yes, even those who do things that make it hard to love them. Children need to know that their parents love them—no matter what happens.

How can you show your kids you love them?

- a pat on the back
- a hug
- putting your arm around their shoulders
- a smile
- a kiss

It is also important to say to your kids, "I love you." You may find it hard to do that. It is hard for some parents. But those words sound so beautiful to children. Watch a child's face light up when you say, "I love you."

Find different ways to show your love to your children. Say it in words at least one time. Watch your child's face when you say it. The more you say it, the easier it is to say again and again and again.

Home Activity #5 Bedtime Routine

Remember when you were a child. What was bedtime like in your family? Was it a positive time? Did someone say "I love you"?

What was your bedtime routine?_____
_____
_____
How did you think and feel? _____
_____
_____
What do you do with your child at bedtime? _____
_____
_____
How can you make it better? _____
_____
_____
What happened after you made changes in your child's bedtime routine? _____
_____

Bedtime is a special time to say "I love you." Write down the different ways you show love to your children.

Child #1 name_____

What did you say or do? _____

_____

What did your child say or do?_____

_____

Child #2 name_____

What did you say or do? _____

_____

What did your child say or do?_____

_____

Child #3 name_____

What did you say or do? _____

_____

What did your child say or do?_____

_____

VIDEO PRACTICE 1

Scene #1: Sara

What did the child feel? _____
_____
_____

What could you say? _____
_____
_____

Scene #2: Zack

What did the child feel? _____
_____
_____

What could you say? _____
_____
_____

Scene #3: Ramon

What did the child feel? _____
_____
_____

What could you say? _____
_____
_____

Scene #4: Ben

What did the child feel? _____

_____

_____

What could you say? _____

_____

_____

Scene #5: Jade

What did the child feel? _____

_____

_____

What could you say? _____

_____

_____

Listen to what your child is feeling. ▶

Scene #6: Janelle

What did the child feel? _____

_____

_____

What could you say? _____

_____

_____

Scene #7: Sara

What did the child feel? _____

_____

_____

What could you say? _____

_____

_____

Scene #8: Zack

What did the child feel? _____

_____

_____

What could you say? _____

_____

_____

Scene #9: Ramon

What did the child feel? _____

_____

_____

What could you say? _____

_____

_____

Scene #10: Jade

What did the child feel? _____

_____

_____

What could you say? _____

_____

_____

**Help your
child decide
what to do.** ▶

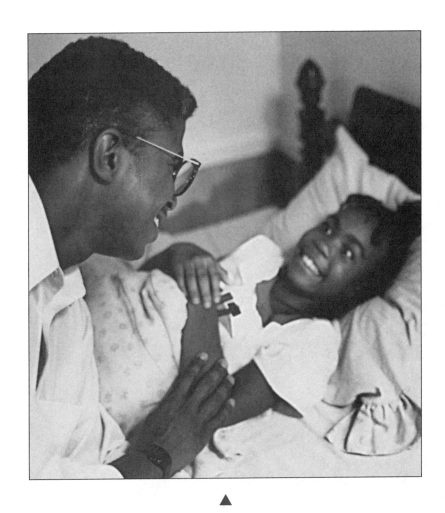

▲

"I love you" are the three most important words
your child can hear.

Chapter 6

The Active Family

We said that children are equal in the family. They are equal in 2 important ways:

1. They deserve respect
2. They can say what they think and feel

If this is true, how can they act like equals? The best way is by talking together. In an "active family," everyone is equal. Everyone can talk about his or her needs. Everyone works together to solve problems. Here are three ways your family can talk together:

- family talks
- solving problems together
- family meetings

Parents should talk to the family about the meetings. No one should be forced to attend. Talk about the good things that will happen in the meeting.

Meetings should include:

- parents
- children
- any other people who live with the family

What if there is only one parent? Everyone who lives together is a family. This includes grandma and grandpa.

Family Talks

These are times the whole family gets together to talk about one thing. Some examples are:

- honesty
- sadness
- alcohol & other drugs

- dating
- privacy
- respect

Talk about what interests you and your family. Here are some suggestions for your next family talk:

 Think about your topic. If the topic is sadness, you can say: "This week let's talk about sadness. Do you remember the movie we saw last night? Why was the boy sad?"

 Think of questions your family can talk about. Sometimes, it is hard for people to talk about certain things. Have some questions ready to keep the talk going.

 Examples:
- How do we know if someone is sad?
- When have you felt sad?
- What do you do when you feel sad?

 This is a time to teach your children "values." Write down things you want your children to know. This is very important if you are talking about drugs or sex. You can also bring books, videos and magazines to share with the family.

Solving Problems Together

Helping our children learn to solve problems gives them tools for success. The whole family can work on a problem. Children learn to cooperate in a group. Solving problems can happen every week or only when needed.

How Do You Talk About a Problem?

1. Everyone must understand the problem.

 Example:
Tyrone has a problem. Everyone listens while he is

talking. Some of his brothers and sisters ask questions until they understand. Then his Dad says, "So we all agree that Kim borrowed Tyrone's favorite jacket without asking. Then someone stole the jacket from her."

2. Next, try to think of different ways to handle the problem. Ask each person to talk. Ask, "What can we do about this problem?" Keep a list of the different ideas.

Every idea is important. No one should be laughed at or put down because of a "silly idea."

3. Then pick 1 or 2 ideas that most of the family agrees on and talk about them. Talk until you all agree on one way to handle the problem.

Example:
One idea was to have Kim pay Tyrone for the jacket. Another idea was for Mom and Dad to pay for Tyrone's jacket.

4. Now you act on it.

Example:
The family decided that Kim should pay for Tyrone's jacket since she took it without permission. She will use her allowance and earn extra money doing chores for the neighbors.

Family Meetings

This meeting can include a family talk or solving problems together. Decide on a time and place that is good for everyone.

Sunday afternoon is a good time for the Smith family. Everyone is together. They can look at what happened last week. They can plan what will happen next week.

What Do You Do at a Family Meeting?

The first meeting should be short. Use it to plan a picnic or a trip to the zoo. Or decide on something fun to do after the meeting. Each meeting will be a little different because of what you will talk about.

One parent should be the leader at the beginning. But once the family gets used to the meetings, each family member can have a turn.

What To Talk About

1. Thank each other for special things that happened:
"Sue, you did a great job on that math test."

"Dad, thanks for helping me fix my bike."

"Grandma, your apple pie was the greatest."

2. What about the problems the family talked about last week? Do you need to talk about them again this week?

3. This is a good time to talk about family money. Give the kids their allowance. Talk about a trip that may be coming up

and how much it will cost. Do you have money problems?
Ask the family for ideas or help.

4. Are there new problems or good news anyone wants to share? Is the family planning a special project?

5. After you end the meeting, do something together. Go outside to play together. Or have a special treat like ice cream. It is important to enjoy time together as a family.

How Do You Know What To Talk About?

You can keep a piece of paper taped to the refrigerator. It can say: "Meeting." Whoever has a problem can write it on the paper. At the meeting, you talk about each item on the paper.

Example:
Child: "Dad, my school is going on a trip and I need some money."

Dad: "I see. Well, Mark, why don't you put it on the meeting list? We will talk about it at this week's family meeting."

Things To Remember About All Meetings

For family talks, solving problems, or family meetings remember the following:

1. **Every person has the right to speak.** This includes small children. Your children will not be excited about the meetings if they think you will be telling them what to do. They will be more excited if they know they will be able to talk. Let them talk about what they like, do not like and problems they have. They need to feel that they will be heard. Everyone should have a chance to talk.

2. **It is important that everyone share what they think and feel about each problem.** Be sure each person has a chance to speak. The family needs to hear all the feelings—even the

negative ones. Parents should not react when their children talk about unpleasant feelings or "different" ideas. Children have to feel safe in sharing their thoughts and feelings.

3. **Everyone should agree on what should be done about the problem.** This does not mean taking a vote. This means everyone talks about the problem and their feelings. They should agree on the solution. What if the family can not all agree on what to do? You can wait until the next meeting and

talk about it again. If something must be done immediately, the parent can decide on the answer.

4. Once you make a decision at the meeting, do not change it. If some family members complain about it, say, "We will talk about it at the next family meeting. But, until then, we made that decision and we will act on it."

5. Parents are still the parents. Having family meetings does not mean parents always do what the children want to do. Sometimes parents will make a decision and tell the children about it at the family meetings. But always let them tell you how they feel and think about the decisions. This is part of the sharing process. It makes the decisions easier for the children to understand.

Home Activity #6 Being Part of The Family

Let your children know they are part of a family. Your "family" may have 2 parents, 1 parent, a stepfather or stepmother. It does not matter. Be sure all your children feel like they belong.

Here are some ways you can do this:

1. **Plan lots of "family" things.**
   Go to the movies together, rent a video everyone likes, pop popcorn and have a popcorn party, have a story time together.

2. **Talk about "our family."**
   "I am so proud of our family."

   "Our family is really growing."

   "Mrs. Jones has invited our family to her house for dinner."

3. **Start doing things the same time each week, each month or each year together.**
   "Every Saturday night, we pop popcorn and watch a movie together."

"Each month, we go to the park and have a picnic. We always have chocolate cake and ice cream. If the weather is bad, we go to a restaurant instead."

"Every year, we put up our Christmas tree the week before Christmas. Everyone is there to help decorate the tree. Then we sit around the tree and sing Christmas carols."

You and your family are the most important part of your child's world.

The Office of Substance Abuse Prevention (OSAP) has 10 roles parents can play to help prevent drug use in your children.

1. Be a good role model. Do not use drugs.

2. Share what you know about tobacco, alcohol and other drugs with your child.

3. Make a "no use" rule—no use of illegal drugs by any family member.

4. Encourage your child to play a sport or find a hobby. Plan family fun time.

5. Teach your child to say "no" to alcohol and other drugs.

6. Know where your children are. Tell them when you expect them home.

7. Join with other parents for support and new ideas.

8. Know how to tell if your children are using drugs.

9. Get medical help fast if your child is sick from drugs.

10. Control your own feelings. Do not get angry. Do not give up.

NOTES

NOTES

NOTES

NOTES

Active Parenting Publishers has additional resources to help parents with

Parenting Skills

Self-Esteem Development

&

Loss Education

For more information, write:

810 Franklin Court, Suite B
Marietta, GA 30067